Understand And Break Free From Your Own Limitations

MATTHEW BRIGHTHOUSE

Copyright © 2017

Table of Contents

INTRODUCTION..3

1 THE FINE LINE BETWEEN STRENGTH AND WEAKNESS 6

2 LEARN TO REIN IN HONESTY 15

3 LEARN TO RELAX AND GO WITH THE FLOW/LEARN TO AVOID PUTTING UNNECESSARY PRESSURE ON YOURSELF 19

4 LEARN TO LET GO WHEN DATING 25

5 LEARN TO APPRECIATE THE DIFFERENCE BETWEEN OPINION AND FACT 30

6 LEARN TO UNDERSTAND THAT NOT EVERYTHING HAS TO MAKE SENSE 33

CONCLUSION...35

Introduction

If you have taken the Briggs-Myers Personality Test and your result stated an ISTJ personality type, you are in good company. ISTJs make up an abundant part of the population, with an estimated 13% standing alongside you. Such celebrities and people of importance who are in your gang include: Robert De Niro, Natalie Portman, Queen Elizabeth II, George Washington, Sean Connery, and Pope Benedict XVI.

The fact that you are an abundant personality type, doesn't make you in any way predictable, because as an ISTJ you are certainly someone who will not stop until they have achieved what they set their mind to. You are someone who is fiercely determined, someone who can be depended upon, and someone who is loyal and family-orientated in your relationships. Overall, you are a great person to have on side.

Of course, every personality type has its upside and downsides, and the whole point of this book is to help you celebrate the positives, and even develop them further, whilst addressing the possible negatives, and turning them around. If you can do this, you will certainly become a well-rounded, fully-developed person in your own right! Understanding your weaknesses is a sign of a mature individual, and accepting them means you are determined to continually develop yourself.

It's quite likely that when undertaking the test, you may have struggled with different options. This is because nobody is 100% a particular personality type, and we all exhibit certain traits of the surrounding types. For this reason, if you notice you are continually nodding towards a different type's traits, then certainly read into that type too. This means that you can give yourself a true personality MOT. This will also give you all the information you need to discover your true self, and really go to work on your own self-development journey.

When reading about the negatives of your personality type as an ISTJ, don't become down heartened. Everyone has negative traits, and if you don't have these, you're not human! The key is to recognise them and work towards minimising their impact. There isn't one personality type out there that is 100% perfect, and you should never aim to be either. Personal development advice can appear harsh at times, but it is never intended to be that way, and is always intended to be useful and to hit home. You are someone who is so logical it can be difficult to see another way to think or feel, but the aim of this book is to show you that development is possible if you open up your mind to another way.

We will start in our first chapter by explaining exactly what an ISTJ personality type is about, giving you important information on what makes you tick. We will then move onto your strengths, celebrating those, before talking about your possible weaknesses. From there, we will work to push forward your strengths even more, and correct your weaknesses, turning them into positives.

So, are you ready for your ISTJ development journey? Grab a pen and paper, remember to make notes as you go through the chapters, and go back over any which don't immediately call out to you as a person. You may not display every single facet of being an ISTJ, but it is likely that it is in there somewhere, and if you can recognize it, pull it out, and develop it, you're well on your way to reaching your end goal.

1
The Fine Line Between Strength and Weakness

As human beings, we are fundamentally flawed. This isn't a bad thing, because perfection is quite frankly boring and impossible! The important thing however is your awareness of this, and to do something about changing your weaknesses into strengths. Development comes about when we analyse ourselves, appreciate the good, recognize the bad, and do something about both. We can begin to enhance ourselves and improve our lives. You love to learn, so this journey should be a great task for you, and one which you can use your fierce dedication to conquer.

As an ISTJ you are an introvert. You are someone who thinks a lot, someone who listens a lot, and someone who is determined to succeed, no matter what. You love to meet your targets and goals, giving yourself a hard time when you don't quite manage it. You are honest to a fault, and sometimes you are a little too honest! As a friend and lover, you are family orientated and loyal. Overall, you're a great person to know! You are someone who will never let down the ones you love, and they feel that to their very core.

Your personality type is known as the Logistician. This means you are a great thinker, and you have a powerful and packed mind. You are a great problem solver, and that means you are also fantastic for advice. You may find that your friends and family often come to you when they have an issue they need to be solved. You can however come across a little cold and aloof, but this changes when people get to know you. All of this is because you simply don't have time for time wasters, so you hold yourself back for the ones who are worth knowing the real you. You can tire yourself out on occasion with the amount of thinking and problem solving you do, and this is something you need to be careful of, and watch out for. We will talk about that in more detail later, to flag up any potential issues.

You might be wondering what ISTJ stands for.

- I – Introvert
- S – Sensing
- T- Thinking
- J – Judging

Let's explore those one by one, as these make up the fundamental building blocks of your personality type overall.

Introvert
You are not someone who is likely to push themselves forward into the limelight without having some reservations about it. You prefer to be in the background, working to make the show tick along, without failure. You are a great listener, and you give great advice. You are not someone who is loud, and instead, you are a thinker, a quiet person who can be depended upon. We mentioned that Queen Elizabeth II is an ISTJ personality type, and she sums up this type really well. The Queen is not a loud person, but she has a presence, she is someone of importance simply by her demeanour. Just because you are quiet

and introverted, doesn't mean that you are a wallflower; you can actually be a real force to be reckoned with when you feel passionate about something you have thought long and hard about.

Sensing
You have a great intuition that can be relied upon, however this is entirely based on fact and logic, and not on emotion or sixth sense – you don't believe in sixth sense, and you have a hard time recognising how your emotions can dedicate your behaviour to a large degree.

You are a dependable person, someone who never lets down another person, and someone who never lets a problem go unsolved. Your mind is a hotbed of facts and figures, and you work tirelessly to meet your deadlines. Your logical mind rarely rests, which can lead to burnout from time to time. This is something that you, as an ISTJ, need to keep in mind, as any perceived failing on your part will be met with your own severe self-judgement. As we mentioned before, we will cover this in detail later on, to allay any worries.

Thinking
ISTJs are all about the mind, as we have mentioned. You are a logistician, you are a thinker, and you are someone who loves to examine an issue from all sides, before coming up with the best possible way to meet it. You are likely to enjoy problem solving, and you are likely to be in a job which is more academic, than creative. Whilst you enjoy creative pastimes, as a career, you prefer something which you can get your

teeth into, preferably with facts and figures – you thrive on logic and hard truth.

Judging

We mentioned earlier that as an ISTJ you can sometimes come over to other people as cold and a little aloof. Unfortunately, your personality type is prone to being a little judgemental. You consider opinion to be fact, and if someone doesn't really relate to your opinion, you don't have much time for it. This is a point to work on, but it is something which can easily be developed. On the plus side, as an ISTJ, you love to grow, and constructive criticism is something you welcome, for development reasons.

If you can learn to be a little more open to the opinions of others, you will be able to turn one of the personality type's biggest weaknesses into a major positive. It is hard to deliver such a weakness without sounding harsh, but as we go through this book, remember that any mention of this weakness is not done with negativity in mind, but with growth in mind instead. You are not a cold-hearted person, you are someone who loves deeply and is fiercely protective, you simply hold logic in such high regard that it can sometimes get in the way, especially to those who aren't so logically minded.

That is the ISTJ in a nutshell, but obviously, there is much more to you than that! You have a wealth of knowledge within that brain of yours, and that means you also have strengths and weaknesses that we need to explore. Let's start with the good stuff!

ISTJ Strengths

A person of integrity and dedication.
One of the main strengths of an ISTJ is the sheer amount of will and dedication that is ingrained in your personality type. You do not like to fail, and you put all your time and effort into ensuring you succeed. You are also a person of integrity and you can be relied upon to be honest and uphold good manners at all times. If you come across someone who is lazy, or doesn't put all their effort into a job they said they would do, you have no time for them; this is a reflection of your hard-working nature.

Very practical and logical
Your logical mind doesn't have time for 'out there' creative thinking, and you much prefer to stick to the facts to complete something, or solve a problem. For that reason, you are relied upon to get the job done by your employer or your colleagues. You are likely to have a very strong, reliable reputation in your workplace, and you are likely to be held in high esteem.

Rarely jumps to conclusions
You are not someone who jumps to extreme conclusions or makes rash judgements, because you prefer to consider the facts first. You are not overtly emotional, so you can make judgements based on the issue at hand, rather than relying upon emotions which may be out of control in the heat of the moment. You however do not tend to understand the situations in life which don't make much sense, because of that logical mind. If you can learn to appreciate the magic of life, the things which really

don't adhere to fact, then you will conquer a big weakness of your personality type.

Very honest and to the point
You can always be relied upon to tell the truth. You are not someone who fabricates stories or uses their imagination very much. You are direct, sometimes a little too much, and this is something we are going to talk about in more detail later on. Honesty is a great strength, because you will never go far wrong when you tell the truth. On the flipside, you can be a little too honest from time to time, which is something to work on in your personal development journey, and something we will discuss shortly in more detail.

Determined, meets deadlines
You do not fail often when it comes to deadlines, because you are so determined to succeed. Again, this places you in high regard in your working life. The downside is that you can beat yourself up a little if you do miss a deadline, albeit rarely. Learning to let go a little is something to work on, and understanding that life can get in the way sometimes, at no fault of your own, or anyone else's.

Calm under pressure
In a pressured situation, you can be relied upon to deliver. You don't flap or worry, and you don't get stressed when under the cosh. You consider the facts and you use your logic to get to the bottom of a situation, keeping your emotions at bay. In an emergency, you are the guy or girl for the job! You will assess calmly, come up with a plan of action, and you will carry everyone through without event.

Flexible in work and life
You can turn your hand to anything, and this makes you a very flexible and useful person to have around the workplace and at home. If you see a job that needs doing, you will assess it logically and you will solve it, no questions asked.

A responsible person who can relied upon
You don't let people down, especially when you have agreed to carry out a job or task. You are highly regarded for your reliability in all areas of your life. As a partner, you are never going to make your other half feel like you don't have their back, or that you are likely to disappear at any time – you are Mr or Mrs stability, and a more emotional person, if you can connect with their illogical side, will find true peace with you.

ISTJ Weaknesses

Stubborn
An ISTJ is known for being a little stubborn. This may be that you don't readily admit if you are wrong, or if you think a situation could be better handled a different way. Your pride can sometimes come before a fall, so learning to let go of situations a little and go with the flow to a certain degree, is something that will serve you well in terms of self-development.

Can be too honest, bordering on insensitive
We mentioned in our introduction section and throughout this chapter that as an ISTJ, the first impression people can sometimes have of you is somewhat cold. This isn't the real you, and when they get to know you they see this. Having said that, you

don't help yourself sometimes by being a little too honest! Honesty is a great trait to have, because as we mentioned, you will never go wrong if you are honest, but there is a fine line between being honest to the point of insensitivity, and simple honesty.

Always goes by the rules, a little too much
You like order, you like everything in its place. This is no bad thing, because at least that way everyone knows where they stand when working and living with you. On the other hand, however, we need to mention what we have already touched upon – learning to go with the flow. This will certainly help you relax, and will help others see you as less uptight, and more for the chilled-out person you can be on occasion.

Can be judgemental
When we talked about what ISTJ actually stands for we mentioned judgement as one of the key facets of this personality type, so it's no surprise that a weakness is that you can be judgemental. Again, you believe your opinion is right, and sometimes that means not understanding that the opinions of others are equally as valid as yours. Learning to accept that opinion isn't necessarily fact is a good starting point to working on this weakness.

Puts too much pressure on themselves/blames themselves unnecessarily
As an ISTJ you can be your own worst enemy sometimes! Things do go wrong on occasion, and it isn't necessarily your fault. You tend to blame yourself if a deadline isn't met, even if the situation was out of your control. Piling too much pressure on

yourself isn't a good thing, and whilst it is certainly admirable that you are trying your best and being so dedicated, it's okay to give less than 110% sometimes, and it's okay for things to go wrong too – such is life! Embrace the unexpected and you will notice a calmer sense of yourself.

Can be a little too reserved when dating

ITSJs aren't necessarily shy, and you probably won't class yourself as shy either. The chances are however, that you are quite reserved instead. This could mean that when you are trying to find a special someone in your life, you find it hard to bring the wall down at first. We will cover this in one of our future chapters, but learning to let go a little when dating is a key factor for ISTJs. This will mean that you find dating much more fun, and that you are likely to find that special person in your life much easier too. Once you do find the right person for you, you are likely to build a successful long-term relationship that is mutually beneficial and fulfilling to the two of you.

As you can see, there is no weakness there that can't be worked upon! You have a lot of strengths as an ISTJ, strengths which other personality types will be envious of. Of course, you have weaknesses too, because you're human. The key is to work on those weaknesses, to develop and improve yourself over time.

So, now you know what kind of work you have in front of you, it's time to get practical! Each chapter is going to focus on a weakness that is common in your personality type, aiming to give you help and advice to flip it around into a strength.

2
Learn to Rein in Honesty

Honesty is always the best policy. How many times have you heard that saying? It's true; in fact, honesty will see you through so many situations in life. For that reason, your strength of being honest is a great one to have.

The flipside?

You can be *too* honest.

There is nothing wrong with telling the truth, in fact, it is to be encouraged. What you need to be careful of however is that you are not insensitive when you deliver the truth. Not everyone wants to hear the cold, hard truth sometimes, and whilst you are certainly not intending to hurt anyone's feelings, because that is not part of your personality, you might not realise you're doing it.

What you need to remember here is that if someone doesn't want to hear the truth, that's their personal choice. You know the truth, that's all you need to know at the end of the day. You may become annoyed or frustrated that you can't get the facts over to them, but not everyone is open to it.

So, how can you tell the truth and ensure that everyone is aware of what they need to be aware of, but in a sensitive way?

The bottom line is that as an ISTJ, you are someone who doesn't primarily deal with emotions first, you deal with facts first and foremost. That means you may not understand someone who is more emotionally charged than you are. You are a logical person, you deal with facts, and if someone isn't listening to you, it's easy for you to lose all tolerance. Learning how to get your point across, i.e. the truth, without hurting anyone's feelings is down to the way you say it.

Now, we have to reiterate here that you certainly do not mean to hurt anyone when you speak the truth. As we said, you may not even realise you've done it. So, when you have something you need to say, think carefully before you speak, and try and put yourself in the position of the person you're speaking to.

It really does depend on what it is you're telling them, i.e. is it something about them and their personal life? Is it something about work? Is it something they are going to be angry or upset about? If it is a sensitive issue, then choose your moment wisely, and be sure to think for a few seconds before you do it.

For instance, you might think you're being totally open and transparent by telling someone that their dress doesn't suit them. You might think that you'd want to know if you were wearing something that wasn't the best it could be, and you have no idea why your friend is tearing up.

Alternatively, you are part of a team at work and one of your team mates simply hasn't delivered the work on time that they promised. This is one of your pet peeves – you have no tolerance for laziness or those who don't meet their requirements. Because you are someone who always goes out of their way to tick the box you're supposed to, you simply don't understand why someone else hasn't done the same. How do you deliver the news?

In both situations, it's about choosing your time and your words. Once you start to think before you tell the truth, you will probably find that it is something you do automatically in the future. For instance, instead of the words just flying out of your mouth, you will think about it before you say it. This is going to cut down on any instances that could hurt someone's feelings unintentionally, and improve this common ISTJ weakness. Approaching the situation in a way that makes it clear to the other person that you are giving constructive criticism and not just general criticism is very important. Finish off the speech with a positive, something that will remain with them. This is how you give honest feedback, without being rude or insensitive.

Another question to ask yourself is this – do they really need to hear it? Will it do them any good? If not, just don't say it; you won't get any thanks for it anyway. Sometimes it's a case of the least said, soonest mended, even if you don't know that what you're saying is wrong.

At the end of the day, as an ISJ, your honesty is both a blessing and a curse, and if you can use it for good, this is a very positive quality to have. Never hold back if you truly believe something needs to be said, but ensure that you deliver the news in the most sensitive of ways possible.

3
Learn to Relax And Go With the Flow/Learn to Avoid Putting Unnecessary Pressure on Yourself

You are a hard-working soul, you are someone who works tirelessly to get the job done and you take great pride in what you do. That's a seriously positive quality to call your own. There is a downside coming however – sometimes as an ISTJ, you have a tendency to try and do too much, to the detriment of yourself.

You do not have to do all of the work yourself, you do not have to take on the world and succeed every single time. You are not Superman or Wonder Woman, you are a human being who deserves time off just as much as the next person, personality type or not.

Burnout is a very real possibility with an ISTJ personality type, because the pressure you put on yourself to succeed time and time again can be debilitating over a prolonged period. Of course, 99% of the time you do the job well and on time, but when you don't, for whatever reason, you really do take it super personally.

Now, there is something that will help you out a lot – it's called the flow.

Learning to go with the flow is something that will not only make you calmer and more relaxed about everything in your life, but ironically, it will probably make situations easier, because you're not trying to control them. When you let go of the reins a little, everything moves the way it is supposed to, and sometimes in a better way than before. Trying to control something and steer a ship in a direction it simply doesn't want to go in, can cause stress and overall it just won't work out. You can try until you are blue in the face, use as much logic as you can muster up, but some situations just aren't there for the solving. This isn't your fault!

Having too much on your plate can be debilitating and it can lead to stress. Burnout is a serious thing, i.e. it can affect your health, relationships, and your work overall. You need to learn that you are not responsible for every single thing that goes on in your workplace or in your life, and that you can surrender control or responsibility to others on occasion.

So, how can you learn to control that innate need to want to do everything yourself?

- Give yourself time off
- Make sure you leave the office/workplace on time
- Switch off when you go home
- If something doesn't work out, simply accept it, move on, and try and do better next time
- Remember that teams share responsibility, it doesn't all fall on you

- Incorporate exercise into your life, it will give you something else to focus on
- Take up yoga – ideal for relaxation
- Consider trying meditation to bring everything into perspective

These are all ways you can learn to go with the flow a little more in life in general.

Ironically, trying to do everything and putting this amount of pressure on yourself to do well is actually an enviable trait in a strange way. You want to succeed and you want to please people – that means you want to better yourself and make things work out for you and those around you. You should pat yourself on the back for that thought and drive. You need to put yourself first however, because the only person you can rely on totally in this life is you. On top of this, if you're putting yourself under unnecessary stress then you are not going to be in the best health or headspace for current or future tasks.

It isn't easy to totally let go of the reins if you're not used to it, because you may suddenly begin to panic that the job isn't going to be done, or that someone else will do it wrong. Realise that for the first few times you do this, yes, you're going to feel worried, but it will pass and get easier. A team works together and it shares responsibility – when things go well, you all get a pat on the back; when things go wrong you all share the rap and make it better next time. This is just life, and the mechanics of team work.

No man (or woman) is an island, and you cannot possibly do everything yourself. Realise this fact, make peace with it, and understand that perceived failure can be used as a learning tool for the next time. Will you smash it on the following occasion? Of course you will, you're an ISTJ!

How to Recognise Undue Stress

We need to give a little nod to stress here because we have talked in depth about how an ISTJ puts so much pressure on themselves. The thing is, because you're so hard-wired to succeed and you try so hard, you probably don't realise you're under stress or displaying classic signs of stress.

There are physical signs and there are mental signs to look out for. You may not see these yourself, so perhaps ask a friend or loved one to check you over from time to time!

Common signs of stress include:

- Frequent headaches
- Overthinking
- Not being able to switch off when you go home
- Disturbed sleep pattern – this can be either wanting to sleep all the time or not sleeping much at all
- Constant tiredness
- Disrupted appetite
- Weight changes, either increase or decrease
- Palpitations
- Anxiety
- Shallow breathing
- Sweating

- Finding that you are becoming ill easily, e.g. you're picking up common colds a lot easier than you normally would
- Worst case scenario thoughts
- Feeling overwhelmed
- Possible depression or low mood

If you notice that you are showing any of these signs regularly then you need to stop and take a look at what it is that is making you stressed out. As an ISTJ it is likely that you are simply trying to do too much on your own, or you are beating yourself up internally for a perceived failing, that probably wasn't a failing at all.

Learning to put things into perspective will help you, and this is where meditation can be a very useful tool. You don't need to learn how to chant or understand how it all works too much to really reap the benefits, you simply need to learn how to calm the constant noise in your head. If you can do that, you will gain a sense of calm and serenity, which will focus your mind on the most important things, and stop the chatter about things that don't really matter.

Exercise is another very useful tool for stress, and as an ISTJ, you will find that getting out into the Great Outdoors an combining it with exercise will help you to calm the constant logic your mind is searching for. Learning to appreciate the wonder of the world, away from how it all works and makes sense, is something that you will gain a lot of benefit from.

You Are Not Uptight ...

A quick last note on this chapter, as we have covered a lot of ground here. We have lumped these two subjects together because they are so closely related and interchangeable, but one thing we need to address is this – as an ISTJ you are certainly not uptight. This is a slice of reassurance for you, because an inability to let go and go with the flow could lead you to that conclusion.

The fact remains that you are an introvert and you are reserved, which means you are quiet and held back; this doesn't mean you are controlling or uptight. Learning to let go and allow life to take you where it leads is a skill which needs practice, a muscle that needs to be flexed regularly in order to make it easier to use on a daily basis. Make this your aim in life – the flow will really allow you to become a calmer and more open-minded person, away from everything having to make logical, factual sense.

4
Learn to Let Go When Dating

ISTJs are reserved types. We mentioned that Queen Elizabeth II is an ISTJ and you're not likely to see her partying it up or being 'out there', even if she wasn't royalty and decorum demanded it. Reserved isn't boring however, and it isn't necessarily the sign of someone who is submissive or wallflower-esque. For instance, Robert De Niro, one of modern day's greatest actors is an ISTJ, and he certainly isn't submissive or someone who can be walked over.

No, reserved simply means respectful, quiet, and someone who listens and looks before they speak or act. Reserved people analyse and apply logic, which sums you up perfectly.

Being reserved can get you through a lot of difficult situations in life, but one particular situation which can be troublesome for ISTJs is dating. Yes, matters of the heart, at least the initial part of the deal, can prove to be a little hard for your personality type.

It isn't that you have a problem with meeting new people, and it's not that you don't want to meet a new special someone; in fact, you love to meet new people. No, the problem is that you have a wall up, and you find it hard to drop that wall when you are dating. You may not really understand the whole concept of dating, because you are so family orientated, you want to jump straight to the security side of it, and not the 'what is going to happen' part of the whole deal. Dating isn't logical, it doesn't make factual sense, and that is why you find it hard to really just go with it from time to time Of course, your desire to pair up and be in union pushes you to try, for which you should pat yourself on the back.

The problem is, that 'what is going to happen' part has to happen in order for the progression, or otherwise, to occur. Now, as an ISTJ you are not a control freak, you don't have a tendency to want to know what is going to happen, and you don't mind waiting and seeing, but you want to succeed, and if you feel that you're not going to find love and happiness with someone, you tend to cut your losses rather early. What if that person is similarly held back and needs time to open up? What if that person is a little shy? You need to be patient and give it time, go with it and see where it leads, for better or worse.

We talked in our last chapter about going with the flow, and in romance, you certainly need to do this, in order to find out whether that person is right for you or not. But I do believe learning to trust your gut is also a very important factor when it comes to dating.

In love, ISTJs are very giving, reliable, and dependable partners. You probably know in yourself that you are very family orientated and you crave stability and security. You are not someone who is going to get along well with a person who is overly emotional, someone who takes you on a crazy rollercoaster romance, and you're not going to bond that well with someone who is lazy or who doesn't work hard in life. You want to meet your equal, you want to meet someone with whom you can walk through life and grow old. This is a very romantic and admirable thought process and it is certainly something you can achieve, if you can just learn to let your wall down.

Dating can be nerve-wracking for you and it can be a challenge, because you can't seem to let go of your reserved nature long enough to simply let your true wonderful self shine through. It takes you a little while to warm up to new people, and you have to feel comfortable for your wall to drop. After a few occasions however, if you feel secure with that person, you will easily allow yourself to be, basically, you. Of course, we also mentioned that ISTJs can sometimes appear aloof or cold when you don't know them, and this doesn't work so well when trying to make a great first impression on a potential mate. Being aware of this and trying to adapt to the situation is key.

Now, how can you learn to drop that wall and be less reserved when dating? How can you make a great first impression, without falling into your safety zone of being slightly cold?

If you are actively on the lookout for the new Mr or Mrs Right, how about asking a close friend or family member to set you up with someone they think would fit? This gives you a little more security, because you're not meeting a random person in a bar or online, you're meeting a mutual contact, someone who your friend feels you would get along with. This should mean you share the same opinions, interests, or perhaps you share common outlooks on life in general. Your friend can also give a little background information on you, so they know that perhaps you're a little reserved at first – it all works!

Go along to this date with an open mind. Talk, be yourself, and simply see what happens. There doesn't need to be success in dating, it simply need to be taken as an experience. If it goes well, great, and if it doesn't? Well, you have something to talk about the next time you see your friend!

Being reserved isn't about being shy, it is about being less inclined to show the world who you are, until you know them better. The key is not to wait too long to reveal yourself – do not hide your light behind a tree, allow it to shine! Smile, make eye contact, nod your head and make the person feel you are listening to them – do not allow aloofness to come into that first contact, otherwise you may push them away before you even get to know them. Be yourself, don't be afraid to go with something that doesn't make logical sense in the moment (more on that later!).

Once you do meet someone you click with, as we mentioned, you are sure to be a truly dedicated partner, and you love long-term relationships. You are not someone who is inclined towards several short partnerships, and you are certainly not a one-night stand kind of guy or girl. You crave security and that means family life. Remember – dating takes time, and you need to dedicate the right amount of time and effort to it. We promise it will be worth it in the end, and they are sure to revel and feel totally at home in your dependable, reliable nature. The world needs more of that kind of feeling in a relationship, when we really open ourselves up and be vulnerable – you are a true shining example of how to make another person feel safe and at home.

5
Learn to Appreciate The Difference Between Opinion And Fact

We mentioned in an earlier chapter that you can sometimes find it difficult, as an ISTJ, to deliver the truth without being a little insensitive at times. Again, you never mean for this to be the case, it can sometimes just be the way the truth is delivered, or the fact that you don't have time or patience for those who are lazy or incompetent.

It may sound harsh, but that is certainly not the aim. Truth is good, and with a little tweaking in approach, as we mentioned, it can be done without any hurt feelings. Now, the next point to address is the difference between opinion and fact.

One of the main weaknesses of an ISTJ is that you sometimes mix up the difference between the two. Opinion is not a logical fact, it is not proven, and it is not the gospel. Fact however is.

Opinion is the way you think, something you believe to be true. Opinion doesn't have to be based on a science it doesn't have to be based on data or numbers, and it doesn't have to be something that is definitely true. It is something you, as a person, believe. Now, it is totally normal to talk about your opinion, and even to debate it with someone else. Healthy debate opens minds, because it means you can find a new outlook on something, and maybe even tweak your own opinion.

Our life experiences and conditioning from a young age determine our beliefs. Where we are today is a result of our beliefs and actions over a period of time. Have you considered challenging certain beliefs that you have? It's possible that something that worked for you 10 years ago, no longer does.

Fact is something entirely different. Fact is literal truth; something there is no arguing with. As you can see, there is a huge difference between the two. ISTJs love fact, because it is logical, it can be worked with, it is reliable, and there is no arguing with it.

Now, as an ISTJ, you can sometimes mix up your opinion with fact. This is because you are so focused on logic, that your opinions are based on logical and true thinking. What you need to realise is that just because something is held dear to you, and because something makes total and utter sense to you, it isn't fact if it is just your belief. Your opinion is no more valid or important than anyone else's and similarly, the opinion of another individual should never trample over the importance of your own.

This can often be a situation in which you can come over as a little judgement and insensitive as an ISTJ. Again, you never meant it to be negative, because you simply can't understand why the other person doesn't share the same thought as you – after all, it makes perfect sense!

The great thing about people however is that they are individual, and that means that opinions are equally as individual. Learn to embrace someone else's opinion and learn to use it as a debating and growth tool, rather than rolling your eyes and telling the other person that their opinion is not valid.

It is a wonderful world we live in with a range of beliefs and opinions. It gives us feedback on what we like or dislike - we can ultimately keep things we do like and change areas that we don't. This will allow us to grow into a better and more fulfilled person.

The point of this chapter is not to be negative in any way, shape or form, and again, we should mention that you hold your opinions in such great regard because they are based on your logic. We know that as an ISTJ you have a very sharp mind, and you love to learn and analyse situations. From that you build your opinions, but always be careful to remember the difference between that and fact.

6

Learn to Understand That Not Everything Has to Make Sense

Again, as an ISTJ, you are super logical in the way you think and feel. You do not believe anything that isn't based on fact and anything which hasn't been proven. Whilst that has many advantages attached to it, you do have to realise that not everything life makes sense. Magic happens occasionally, the unexplained occurs, and sometimes there really is no rhyme or reason. These are the types of occurrences that you struggle with.

The thing is, without wanting to sound all Disney, the things which can't be explained are actually some of the most fascinating things to enjoy. Embracing the magic of life, the things which don't make logical sense, will enhance your life, and will actually help you to understand that major difference between opinion and fact, which we were talking about in our last chapter.

For instance, there have been many times in the past when someone has had an accident and against all odds they survived. If you analysed this logically, there would be no way they would survive, no way they would still be standing today, heart beating and everything; yet, they did, and they're here to tell the tale. How do you explain it? You can't. Perhaps there are examples you can think of in your own life experience?

As an ISTJ, you might tie yourself up in knots trying to understand it and trying to find some logic to explain it, but the bottom line is that there just isn't any. This may drive you made, this may actually annoy you, because where is the logic you seek?

Now, most things in this world do have to make logical sense, and as an ISTJ you manage to find that logic easily. Some things however, they simply don't fit the mould, and these things should be enjoyed. Ironically if you can grasp this thought and really revel in the situations in life which don't make sense, then you can learn to go with the flow much easier too.

We have mentioned that ISTJs struggle with the flow, but if you can try and work this into your mindset, you will find your life much easier. You won't put so much pressure on yourself, and you don't struggle with situations that can't be met. This can all be done with this appreciation of the unexplained.

Of course, we are not talking about believing in the Tooth Fairy or Santa Claus, but we are talking about the small details in life which don't have fact to back them up. If these situations can happen, and if you can believe it yourself, then you will find it easier to accept opinions and views from other people that don't adhere to total logic and fact.

Conclusion

So, there we have it, the positive and negative side of being an ISTJ. Your logical and highly dependable nature is a true quality that needs to be embraced, and you are certainly someone who can be relied upon to not only get a job done, but to be there when you need to be too. Any negative we have mentioned in this book can easily be worked upon, and whilst a lot of the advice isn't practical, it is more mindset related.

Logic doesn't have to work all the time – the world moves in mysterious ways and if you can learn to grasp that thought and go with it, without really trying to analyse it, you will really be able to grasp the small things in life. Ironically, this will allow you to let go of situations that would otherwise have caused you a large amount of stress.

The fact that as an ISTJ you put so much pressure on yourself means that you need to be careful of burn out and stress. You are not someone who can save the world on your own, because nobody can. You need to learn to let go and share responsibility, and to enjoy the things in life which simply don't make sense.

We Are Never Strictly One Type

We are all individuals, and that means that nobody really 100% falls into one personality type. When you took the Myers-Briggs Personality Test you were flagged up as an ISTJ because that is the predominant type you displayed from your answers. You could be

99% ISTJ, or you could be 75%, but overall that dictates the traits you mentioned. Now, what about the other percentage?

You are likely to have shown a few traits from other personality types, and if you want to really understand every corner of yourself, and push your personal development even further forwards, then learning about all the personality types you ring true with, can help you hugely. This can also help you understand the people around you, and that overall helps you too – it's a circle that is in no way vicious, and in many ways hugely beneficial!

The biggest stumbling blocks that you will face as an ISTJ as you try and rectify and develop your weaknesses are:

- Really appreciating the differences between fact and opinion
- Learning to let go and go with the flow
- Learning to not let your honesty be too much

These are the biggest traits that can have a negative side of your personality type, but each of those is a positive too. For instance, fact and opinion opens up debate, and provided you can rein it in and understand that everyone has a valid opinion, you can possibly learn something new.

If you can really learn to go with the flow then your world will open up hugely, but overall, your honesty is your greatest alley and foe. Embrace your honesty, the world really does need more of it, but ensure that you don't take it too far and allow it to hurt people unintentionally.

If there is any part of this book that you are struggling to really understand or grasp, simply go back over it and try the exercises and thought processes we have suggested. This is not an overnight journey, and changing your mindset and adapting to your weaknesses is something which will take time. Having the patience and dedication to go through this journey however is made for you as an ISTJ, because once you get your teeth into a project, you rarely give up until you have succeeded! If you are going to put pressure on yourself to achieve anything in life, make it this project!

Note from the author

Thank you for purchasing and reading this book. If you enjoyed it or found it useful then I'd really appreciate it if you would post a short review on Amazon. I do read all the reviews personally so that I can continually write what people are wanting.
If you'd like to leave a review then please visit the link below:

https://www.amazon.com/dp/B077H5714T

Thanks for your support and good luck!

Check Out My Other Books

Below you'll find some of my other books that are popular on Amazon and Kindle as well. Simply search the titles listed below on Amazon. Alternatively, you can visit my author page on Amazon to see other work done by me.

ENFP: Understand and Break Free From Your Own Limitations

INFP: Understand and Break Free From Your Own Limitations

ENFJ: Understand and Break Free From Your Own Limitations

INFJ: Understand and Break Free From Your Own Limitations

ENFP: INFP: ENFJ: INFJ: Understand and Break Free From Your Own Limitations – The Diplomat Bundle Series

INTP: Understand and Break Free From Your Own Limitations

INTJ: Understand and Break Free From Your Own Limitations

ENTP: Understand and Break Free From Your Own Limitations

ENTJ: Understand and Break Free From Your Own Limitations

OPTION B: F**K IT - How to Finally Take Control Of Your Life And Break Free From All Expectations. Live A Limitless, Fearless, Purpose Driven Life With Ultimate Freedom

Printed in Great Britain
by Amazon